CONDUCTING CHURCH AUDITS:
A Guide for Internal Auditors

Second Edition

CONDUCTING CHURCH AUDITS:
A Guide for Internal Auditors

JEREMY W. ODOM

Big O Publishing Group

© 2016

Conducting Church Audits, 2nd Edition
Copyright © 2016 by Jeremy W. Odom
All rights reserved.

ISBN: 978-0-9970-9562-3

Published by Big O Publishing Group
Natchitoches, Louisiana

The author has worked to ensure that all information in this book is accurate as of the time of publication. As research and practice advance, however, standards may change. For this reason it is recommended that readers evaluate the applicability of any recommendations in light of particular situations and changing standards.

Big O Publishing Group has made every effort to trace the ownership of all quotes. In the event of a question arising from the use of a quote, we regret any error made and will be pleased to make the necessary correction in future printings and editions of this book.

Library of Congress Control Number 2016905442

Printed in the United States of America

Ordering Information:

Special discounts are available on quantity purchases by corporations, associations, educators, and others. For details, contact the publisher at Big O Publishing Group, 431 5th Street, Natchitoches, LA 71457.

U.S. trade bookstores and wholesalers: Please make contact with Big O Publishing Group via email sales@bigopublishinggroup.com.

Contents

1. PURPOSE OF AN AUDIT

This book is intended to be used by an internal auditor or audit committee of a Church belonging to the Louisiana Ministerial Association, Inc. *This audit program is not intended to be and should not be used as a substitute for an external audit conducted by a certified public accountant.* This program is intended to supplement an external audit. It should be used by the internal auditor(s) to help them prepare for an audit conducted by a certified public accountant. By following the instructions contained in this guide, you may be able to reduce the cost and improve the effectiveness of your external audit.

It should be noted that this guide is not to be considered legal or financial advice, nor can it be responsible for the conduct of local audits. Internal auditors should always seek assistance and advice on specific issues from professional accountants and auditors.

The purpose of an audit is the summation of the items presented below:

- Independently verify the reports of the treasurer(s) and financial secretary.
- Follow the money and test how it is treated at different steps.
- Document that donated and earned funds of the congregation have been used as stipulated by the donors.
- Reviews-accounting controls (systems that reduce the possibility of loss, embezzlement or errors).
- Segregation of duties (assurances that more than one person is involved in critical steps in handling money so that there can be checks and balances).

- Reasonableness of systems and procedures in the light of all factors, including the size of the church and its budget.
- Records that show donors' stipulations for the use of gifts made to the local church.

I recommend that an audit be conducted on an annual basis. This is because an audit is "the best way for a local church to protect those persons it elects to offices of financial responsibility from unwarranted charges of carelessness or improper handling of funds. It is in no wise a symbol of distrust." In addition, church committees, treasurers, finance committees, deacons, and other "persons in positions of responsibility are liable for any losses which would have been discovered by an ordinary audit but were not discovered because they failed to have the audit conducted."

Although the primary reason for conducting an audit is to insulate church officers from the suspicion of mishandling of funds, current headlines indicate that mishandling of funds does occur. Much more numerous are the small cases which go unreported. Can this happen in your Church? Unfortunately, it can, and the larger the size of your endowment or your budget, the greater the risk to your Church.

Although most church officers recognize the benefits of having an audit conducted, many still are reluctant to engage professional auditors because of the expense involved. However, given the present volume and complexity of the laws and accounting standards, it should be noted that a professional would most likely save the Church money in the long run. In addition, an announcement to the congregation that an audit has been completed and that all monies and investments are properly accounted for will have a positive impact on stewardship.

An audit consists of a series of procedures done to independently verify the financial statements of the Church. It includes examining, on a test basis, specific information, which supports the amounts and disclosures in the treasurer's financial statement. An audit also includes assessing the accounting principles used by the management of the Church. The purpose of an audit is generally to express an opinion about the treasurer's financial reports.

An audit includes examination of all of the funds of the Church, not only the operating accounts. Thus, all operating accounts, capital and other special funds, endowment and trust funds, assets of Church organizations, investment funds, discretionary funds, and any other assets, liabilities, revenues, and expenses of the Church must be audited. No account should be exempted from examination.

An audit is conducted in three parts – Pre-audit planning, tests of internal controls, and substantive tests of transactions and account balances; the audit should be performed in this order only. The culmination of these tests is the formulation of an opinion on the financial statements (which should consist of at least a statement of the assets and financial statements (which should consist of at least a statement of the assets and liabilities of the church and a statement of the revenues, expenses, and net asset or fund balances of the church). The opinion is expressed in a report, which is issued to the congregation.

The first step of the audit is the planning stage. Pre-audit planning involves obtaining an understanding of the church's financial operations and assembling the various documents that are needed to perform the audit.

Tests of internal controls involve tests of the policies and procedures employed by the church to safeguard assets and to ensure the reliability of the accounting data. The auditor examines the internal controls in order to determine the extent of the tests of the account balances. The better the internal control, the less testing of financial statement account balances is required by auditors.

Finally, substantive tests of transactions and account balances include examination of actual transactions and balances. For instance, the financial statement may indicate a balance of $10,000 in cash. In this stage of the audit, the auditor will examine the bank reconciliations and bank statements and verify that the balance per the bank is properly reconciled to the treasurer's report.

It should be noted that a "review" or "compilation" performed by an independent CPA is not considered an acceptable form of an "audit." Both of these types of engagements are significantly less in scope than an audit performed in accordance with professional standards. A "review" only requires the auditor to perform inquiry and analytical procedures. Confirmation of balances and detailed testing are not performed. A "compilation" is simply the compilation of data provided by the church. No actual testing is performed. Both a "review" and "compilation" offer very limited assurance on the accuracy of the underlying financial statements. For these reasons, neither should be performed in the place of an actual audit (or the recommended procedures outlined in this guide).

In addition, the following information should be present to the audit or finance committee of the church for their consideration:

• Adequacy of insurance coverage.

- Systems for retaining and accessing meeting minutes that have financial implications (i.e. Finance Committee, Trustees, Charge Conferences).

A local church's unique circumstances may suggest that additional steps should be taken. It is important to document the financial processes of your particular local church.

2. SELECTING AN AUDITOR

The type of auditor selected and the type of audit performed at each church each year will be dependent on the amount of funds received by the church. In general, the following guidelines should be used to determine the type of audit that should be performed each year as well as the type of auditor who should perform the audit (i.e., if a certified public accountant firm should be hired to perform the audit or if an independent volunteer will be adequate):

1. For churches that are considered very small (e.g., those with 10 to 20 members and with minimal funding and asset balances), the processes and internal controls in place may vary greatly. For those churches, an independent qualified member of the church or other volunteer from another church can perform audit procedures and evaluate internal controls and report the results directly to the church's finance committee.

   The recommended procedures included in this guide should serve as example procedures that may be performed. Depending on the nature of the church activities and assets, many of these procedures may not be relevant and as such, may not need to be performed. In addition, other procedures may be considered necessary based on the nature and activities of each specific church.

   In addition to the financial transaction procedures, the auditor should assess the design of the church's internal controls. While smaller churches may not have ideal internal controls in place, church leadership should work to implement internal controls in key risk areas to help ensure assets are not misappropriated or misused and errors are detected quickly.

2. For churches with less than $500K in receipts, an independent qualified member of the church or other volunteer can perform audit procedures and evaluate internal controls and report the results directly to the church's finance committee. The recommended procedures included in this guide should serve as the minimum expected financial transaction procedures. Other procedures may be considered necessary based on the nature and activities of each specific church. In addition to the financial transaction procedures, the auditor should assess the design of the church's internal controls.

3. For churches with between $500K and $1M in receipts, the recommended procedures outlined in this guide or a financial statement audit conducted in accordance with generally accepted auditing standards (GAAS) should be completed and reported on by an external Certified Public Accountant (CPA) every three years.

    If the recommended procedures are performed by the CPA, the procedures would be performed as part of an Agreed Upon Procedures (AUP) engagement. As part of either type of engagement, the auditor would be expected to communicate any internal control deficiencies that are identified during the audit procedures.

    In the alternate years, a review similar to number one in this list should be conducted. A volunteer or member of the church could perform and report on the procedures and perform the internal control evaluation.

4. For churches between $1M and $2M in receipts, a financial statement audit conducted in accordance with generally accepted auditing standards (GAAS) should be completed and reported on by an external Certified Public Accountant at least every <u>two</u> years. An agreed upon procedures engagement is not permitted in the place of the GAAS audit.

   Similar to #2 above, in the alternative years when the GAAS audit is not performed, a volunteer or member of the church could perform and report on the recommended procedures and perform the internal control evaluation.

5. For churches with receipts greater than $2M, an external financial statement audit conducted by an independent CPA in accordance with GAAS should be performed <u>every year</u>. Any identified internal control deficiencies should be reported by the independent CPA. An agreed upon procedures engagement is not permitted in the place of the GAAS audit.

   Each of the scope amounts included above should be calculated as the average for each of the last three fiscal years for the church. Further, the applicable procedure or audit reports should be presented within six months of the fiscal year end.

3. THE AUDIT COMMITTEE

The Audit Committee represents the interests of the membership of the church, as well as those of the clergy, the church governing body, and even those of the regional or national ecclesiastical body. The Audit Committee is entrusted to perform a task that none of these individuals or groups can perform, primarily because they do not have access to the financial information and transactions of the church on a daily basis. The members and other interested parties are not in a position to judge the accuracy and fairness of any summarized financial reports which the church produces.

The Audit Committee has the task of attempting to verify the truth and accuracy of the information contained in the church's financial reports, and by expressing an opinion on such information, make them more believable and acceptable to all interested parties. Such credibility can be achieved only if the Committee itself is believable. It is often said that the cornerstone of any audit is *independence*, meaning that the auditors must be unbiased and impartial regarding the material which is the subject of their audit. Only then can they offer a fair opinion on what they have examined.

Perception can be just as important as reality in meeting this test, for an individual may be the most honest and objective person alive, but if the membership of the church *perceives* that person to be biased or to have a vested interest in the subject matter of the audit, any report they might give will not be credible. Thus it is not appropriate for a church's treasurer or financial secretary to serve on the Audit Committee. Certainly these individuals will play a central role in the audit, and they must be readily available to the Committee. The audit and the audit report, however, must be produced by individuals who are not now, and have not been, involved in the accounting or record keeping for the church during the year under audit.

The church and its leadership have a stewardship responsibility to see that the resources made available are used in the service of Christ and in the manner designated by the church leadership and the membership. This responsibility also extends to managing special gifts which may be restricted by the donor, and thus are available only for a specific purpose. A properly functioning Audit Committee will help the church to fulfill it stewardship responsibility by helping to assure that resources have been used in the proper fashion.

The church Audit Committee has a uniquely challenging task because of the environment in which it must operate. Churches are typically, and appropriately, characterized by a high degree of trust among the staff and employees. Nonetheless, prudence dictates that the church leadership must remain ever vigilant in order to fulfill the responsibilities given to it. No individual is above temptation. Even Jesus Himself was tempted by Satan. And yet who among mortals has the strength of Christ to withstand all such assaults?

The Audit Committee is sometimes perceived as superfluous or unnecessary because of the trust placed in the church's treasurer and/or financial secretary. In the vast majority of cases that trust is well deserved. In other cases, the Committee is viewed by those whose work comes under scrutiny as an attempt to discredit or devalue their work. Indeed, the treasurer or financial secretary should not view the Audit Committee as a vehicle by which the church is expressing distrust or suspicion. On the contrary, the Audit Committee in a church should celebrate the good work of the treasurer and financial secretary and hold it up high for all the membership to see!

The objectives of the church Audit Committee are somewhat narrower than those of a public accountant auditing financial statements of a business. Most businesses must conform to a set of required accounting principles when presenting financial statements to the public, and auditors therefore gear their work toward reporting on whether the business' statements are in conformity with such acceptable accounting principles.

For many churches, especially smaller ones generally accepted accounting principles (GAAP) are usually a non-issue. Compliance with such principles would only become important if the church had a need to publish its financial statements to outside parties, such as a lending institution, and was therefore required to have the statements audited by an independent outside auditing firm. Statements prepared for internal use by the church and its members need not conform to generally accepted accounting principles, although they certainly can be so prepared if the church wishes. It is usually much easier for the church to prepare just those statements and schedules which it finds most useful, however.

Since most churches find that the information they need most often revolves around cash receipts and cash payments, the reports they have developed focus on these aspects of the church's operations. Accordingly, the principal objectives of the church Audit Committee will also concentrate on these areas. In general terms, the Committee must be able to satisfy itself that all cash received by the church has been recorded properly and deposited into a bank account where access is limited. Similarly, it should be satisfied that all cash payments have been properly authorized by the appropriate body within the church, properly documented and recorded. Finally, the Committee must be satisfied that all of these receipts and payments are correctly summarized and reported in the annual financial reports of the church, and that the information con-contained therein agrees with the underlying records of the church.

The Audit Committee's responsibilities will extend to other areas as well. For example, if the church has investments in securities such as stocks and bonds, the Committee will seek to assure itself that any purchase or sale transactions during the year have been properly authorized and recorded, and that the list of investments in the year-end financial reports is complete and accurate, properly representing what the church owns at year-end. On the other hand, if the church has any outstanding debts such as mortgages or loans, the Committee will want to assure itself that all required payments have been made during the year, and that the balances reported in the church's financial statements are accurate as of the date of the statements.

There are other areas which should get the Committee's attention too. These include the payroll area where the Committee will want to make sure that all employees and staff are being paid at the rate approved by the church governing body. Additionally, the Committee should satisfy itself that the church has adequate insurance coverage for all of its property and potential liabilities. Also, the Committee may wish to conduct a periodic inventory of the church's property such as office equipment, audiovisual equipment, furniture, and similar items, comparing results with previous inventories to make certain that no assets have become missing.

One final area which should be of concern to the Audit Committee is often overlooked in the rush to "crunch the numbers" in the church's annual financial reports. This area is the daily, weekly, and monthly accounting *practices and procedures* employed in the church, and it is vital to the accuracy of the ultimate financial reports. If the procedures and practices used on an ongoing basis are not sound, there may be errors which will be beyond the ability of the Audit Committee to discover. Items may be overlooked and never recorded, or they may be lost.

It is the validity of the ongoing practices and procedures that will provide some assurance that all events get recorded and nothing is lost along the way. The Audit Committee can be helpful here by reviewing the practices and procedures in use and making constructive suggestions when necessary. To assist in this function, the questionnaires included in this guide that will help the Committee to identify potential weaknesses in the church's accounting practices and procedures.

Throughout the process, the Audit Committee should document its work. All good auditors do this in the form of audit schedules or work papers which form the basis and provide the evidence for the auditor's conclusions. Church auditors should be no different in this regard. You are ultimately going to issue a report on the soundness of the annual financial reports, so you should have a well-documented basis for doing so.

4. PRE-AUDIT PLANNING

For audits performed by a qualified member of the church or other volunteer, the person(s) must obtain access to the following information and materials (at a minimum) during the audit:

1. Copies of all church policies and procedures related to finance and treasury functions and copies of minutes approving those policies.
2. Copies of all minutes from the finance committee, the trustees, the administrative board, the previous charge conference(s), and any other entity.
3. Listing of all bank and investment accounts, including the person authorized to sign on each, and including any special use accounts under the control of the pastor(s) and in the name of the church.
4. All financial statements for each month of the year, plus December of the prior year and January of the subsequent year (a fourteen month period).
5. Bank and investment account statements for the same period.
6. Bank reconciliations for that same period.
7. Original books of entry, which will be the general and subsidiary journals; for those books that are computerized, a print-out of all transactions by account for the entire year.
8. All paid invoices, payroll data and files (including 941's, year-end W-2's, 1099's and transmittal forms), income transmittals and deposit records for the fourteen month period.
9. The Financial Secretary's records and other income records for the same period.

For audits performed by an independent external auditor, similar information will be requested.

The person(s) conducting the audit may obtain access to confidential information and must treat that information accordingly. The auditor's work papers may contain confidential information. These work papers as well as all financial records should be retained for at least seven years in a secure, limited access, storage area.

Before the audit begins, there are certain procedures, which the auditor must do in order to properly plan and perform the audit. First, the auditor must obtain a preliminary understanding of the accounting systems (both manual and computer) that generate significant financial statement items and of related principal internal accounting controls.

The auditors should then obtain copies of the minutes of any committee authorized to receive and disburse monies. Read the minutes with regard to the election of officers, compensation of personnel, bonding of the treasurer, budget approvals, contracts entered into, purchase of items, borrowing of monies, purchase and sale of securities, resolution confirming clergy housing allowance for tax purposes, etc. This should be done before the actual examination of any accounting records. You may need to see the minutes of the previous year if they contain authorizations for expenditures in the year being audited.

Obtain a copy of the previous audit. This will enable you to verify the beginning balances of the assets, liabilities, and net assets. If available, you should also obtain the previous year's management letter. The management letter details past audit findings and provide suggestions on how to improve the church's financial operations.

Obtain a copy of the annual financial statements as prepared and presented by the treasurer.

Review the procedures, which are being used to account for church monies. Identify the individuals with responsibility for financial operations and decisions by name and position and verify with them that all the funds of the congregation have been included in the statements.

Identify all bank accounts and authorized check and withdrawal signers including those under separate treasurers.

Request that all accounting records of all funds be presented together including:

1. Chart of Accounts and Organization Chart
2. General Ledger
3. Cash Receipts Journals
4. Cash Disbursements Journals
5. Bank Statements including all cancelled checks
6. Blank checks that are both in and out of the binder
7. Paid invoices
8. Individual payroll records including Forms W-4 and I-9
9. Federal and State payroll withholding reports
10. Passbooks and evidence of other investments

Perform a preliminary analytical review of the financial statements. This may consist of the current accounts to the previous year balances and to the budgeted amounts. After this is done, arrange a meeting with the Treasurer. Inquire as to any significant variances noted in the preliminary analytical review. Also ask the Treasurer about any matters noted in the reading of the minutes and ask about any other matters, which may have occurred during the year in which you should be aware of before beginning the audit.

As previously discussed, the audit may be performed via the following based on the amounts of the funds received (averaged over the prior three years):

- Procedures conducted by an independent member of the church or volunteer.
- Procedures conducted by an independent accountant hired by the church.
- Financial Statement Audit performed by an independent CPA hired by the church.

For recommended procedure evaluations, the auditor (either a volunteer or CPA) should meet with church leadership (including the finance or audit committee) and determine the procedures to be performed to ensure all necessary financial information is included in the scope of the procedures. It is worth noting that church leadership will be responsible for identifying all financial information and processes to be included in the scope of the procedures. As part of an AUP engagement, the auditor should work to understand the church's internal controls within the processes being audited and then communicate any deficiencies identified during the performance of the procedures.

For financial statement audit engagements, the CPA will conduct the audit in accordance with generally accepted auditing standards to obtain reasonable assurance that the financial statements are not materially misstated. As part of the audit, the CPA will communicate any significant internal control deficiencies identified during the audit.

5. INTERNAL CONTROLS

As part of the audit, it is essential that the internal control structure for receipts and disbursements procedures be reviewed regardless of the size of the church. The internal control structure is the process that assures the local church's operational efficiency and effectiveness, that its financial reporting is reliable, that it is complying with the laws, and that its assets are safeguarded. The internal control process should be in place on paper as well as in practice. Internal control systems that are only policy and are not enforced are no better than having no system at all.

The following guidelines are intended to assist those with financial responsibilities in local churches to identify and implement basic internal control procedures. These minimum standards should be increased for churches with higher volumes of transactions, and should be considered for lower volumes of transactions. Ideally, all local churches will meet these minimum standards and these procedures should be reviewed to ensure practice of each of these during the annual evaluation.

Receipts and Disbursements

- Treasurer and Financial Secretary should not be the same person and should not be in the same immediate family residing in the same household
- Counting team of at least two unrelated persons (I recommend three) should count offerings and document totals – not treasurer and not financial secretary
- Offerings should be deposited the same or next business day

- Offering count details should be given to financial secretary for recording
- Offering totals should be given to the treasurer or financial secretary to record deposit
- The Financial Secretary's deposit log should be compared to the bank statement to verify deposits (by bank reconciliation reviewer)
- At least two persons should be listed as authorized signatures on all accounts. This should also be the case for setting up electronic payments (or EFTs). For EFTs, one of those individuals should be a Trustee or a member of the Finance Committee (other than the Secretary or Treasurer).
- The Treasurer is authorized to make electronic payments of bills. The Treasurer shall maintain support for every electronic payment just as with the support for paper checks.
- Financial policy and authority guidelines should be written and approved by the Finance Committee
- Invoices should be required for all payments from all accounts
- Someone other than the treasurer (with authority by Finance Committee) should approve invoices for payment
- Typically, the Treasurer should make payments only after the invoice is approved. A policy may be implemented where routine, budgeted expenses (i.e., rent/mortgage, electric bill, etc.) may be paid without recurring approval; non-routine expenses must be approved prior to payment.

Reporting and Review

- All accounts should be reconciled monthly
- Someone other than treasurer should review bank reconciliation at least semiannually – including bank statements, invoices, checks written, and financial reports

- The Treasurer should make detailed report of budget and designated fund activities to the Finance Committee at least quarterly

Tax Reporting Requirements

- W-2s must be issued for employees, including pastors, and 1099s issued for nonemployee compensation by January 31 for preceding year (federal law requirement)
- Payroll tax forms and deposits done as required for payroll amount (federal law requirement) - payroll reporting should be completed for the IRS and SSA by appropriate due date for filing method
- Housing allowance or exclusions approved annually and kept on file (federal law requirement)

Other General Requirements

- Prepare list of all church property for insurance purposes - include item description, serial number and value
- Prepare list of safety deposit box contents - update authority as needed - access should be allowed by two unrelated people
- Computer records are backed up and password protected for security
- Ideally, four individuals are required for regular financial procedures: financial secretary, treasurer, person to review and approve invoices and person to review bank reconciliations. It is possible for this to be accomplished with 3 individuals if proper segregation is achieved.

The steps outlined in this section have been compiled into a checklist for easier use during an audit. This checklist is included in the following chapters. When all the audit review steps have been completed, the auditor should review the work done with the church treasurer and financial secretary, endeavor to answer any lingering questions, then consider preparation of the report of the audit.

6. REVIEW & ASSESSMENT OF INTERNAL CONTROLS

In order to properly plan and perform the audit, the auditor must first obtain an understanding of the internal control environment and assess its overall effectiveness. The internal control structure consists of the church's policies, procedures, and commitment to reasonably prevent material errors and irregularities from occurring or going undetected.

Internal control can be described as the overall plan of the church and the methods employed by the church to safeguard assets, ensure the reliability of the accounting data, encourage compliance with established procedures, and promote efficient operations. Good internal controls provide greater assurance that transactions are recorded properly.

The review of the control system must be done by the auditor in order to assess the risk that the financial statements are materially misstated. Thus, if the controls in a particular area are bad, the risk that the account is misstated is higher and more testing in this area may be merited.

An internal control questionnaire is a good way to review the internal controls. You should fill out the questionnaire before the start of the audit. The questionnaire is intended to provide guidance to the auditor, which is used to evaluate the existing system. The normal answer is "yes." However, a "no" answer does not necessarily mean that the church is unauditable or that the control environment is ineffective. It may simply suggest an area of the system that could be strengthened.

In addition, to supplement the questionnaire, a narrative description of the control procedures should be developed to provide documentation of the current review. This narrative should be retained for reference in future evaluations.

After obtaining an understanding, of the control system via a review of the questionnaire and narratives, the responses must be tested to evaluate whether the controls are operating properly.

Internal Control Questionnaire

General: The following items are intended to provide you with general information for an understanding of the over accounting and internal control system.

Question	Yes/No	Comments
Are prior internal control questionnaires available?		
Have recommendations of prior reports on internal controls been implemented?		
Is a complete and current chart of accounts and their respective account numbers, available?		
Is the accounting system using a double-entry bookkeeping method?		

Budget: The development and use of a budget is a critical management tool that will aid in the stewardship and administration of church resources and program.

Question	Yes/No	Comments
Is the budget approved by the Church?		
Are all changes to the budget authorized by the church committee and recorded in the minutes of the meeting?		

Is there a periodic review of the budget by the church committee?		

Reporting: The best accounting system is of little value unless the information is communicated to those responsible. Although there may be variations, there are certain minimum standards to assure adequate communication of the financial information.

Question	Yes/No	Comments
Is a Treasurer's report submitted to the church committee or finance committee each month?		
Is the Treasurer's report presented in sufficient detail to inform the reader as to the nature of the various items of income and disbursements?		
Does the report present the current actual financial data compared with the approved budget?		
Is there periodic reporting, at least quarterly, of all other funds and activities, including designated or restricted funds?		

Cash receipts: Clearly stated policies and procedures regarding the handling of cash and other receipts help not only to protect from loss, but assure that all receipts are properly recorded in the records.

Question	Yes/No	Comments
Are there safeguards to protect the collections from theft or misplacement from the time of receipt until the time the funds are counted & deposited?		
Are the collection receipts counted and deposited so that the deposit equals the entire amount of receipts on a timely basis, i.e., at least weekly?		
Are there at least two unrelated persons responsible for the counting and depositing of the collections?		
Are the persons responsible for counting receipts rotated on a periodic basis?		
Do the counters have a standardized form for recording the deposit information?		
Are the counter's sheets retained and reconciled with actual deposits, and are all discrepancies investigated?		
Is the cashing of checks out of the currency received prohibited?		
Are third party checks returned to donors?		
Are all of the pledge envelopes or other memoranda retained		

and reconciled to the recorded amounts?		
Are all other cash receipts recorded and deposited on a timely basis?		
Are all checks received restrictively endorsed "for deposit only" upon receipt?		
Are there procedures, which will highlight, or bring to someone's attention, the fact that all receipts or income have not been received or recorded?		
Are periodic statements provided to donors of record, i.e., at least quarterly?		
Do acknowledgements of contributions in excess of $250 include a receipt from the donee organization which describes itself as the contemporaneous acknowledgment required by the Internal Revenue Code, and states that, in accordance with Section 170(F)(8)(B), any goods or services provided consist solely of intangible religious beliefs?		
Are all discrepancies investigated?		

Cash disbursements: The following procedures will assist in assuring that all payments are properly approved, recorded, and supported by appropriate documentation.

Question	Yes/No	Comments
Are all disbursements made by check, except for small expenditures made by petty cash?		
Are all checks pre-numbered and used in sequence?		
Is there a clearly defined approval process for all disbursements?		
Are all voided checks properly canceled and retained?		
Are all checks made payable to specified payees and not to cash or to bearer?		
Are all disbursements supported by original documentation?		
Is the original vendor's invoice or other documentation canceled at the time of signature to prevent duplicate payment?		
Is the signing of blank checks prohibited?		
Is the use of a signature stamp or preprinted signatures prohibited?		
Does all supporting documentation accompany checks presented for signature?		
Are all account signers authorized by the church?		
Is more than one signature required for any check?		
If not, do checks for more than		

$500 require more than one signature?		
If signature imprint machines are used, are the keys kept under lock and key except when in use?		
Are all disbursements requiring special approval of funding sources or of the church committee properly documented in the Church committee or Finance Committee minutes?		

Journal entries: Journal entries offer a special opportunity to make adjustments to accounting records. The general journal is just as important a book of original entry as the cash receipts and cash disbursements journals.

Question	Yes/No	Comments
Is there an appropriate explanation accompanying each journal entry?		
Are all journal entries approved by a knowledgeable person of authority other than the person initiating the entry?		
Is adequate documentation maintained to support each journal entry?		

Bank account reconciliation: The monthly reconciliation of all bank accounts is a primary tool for assuring the proper recording and accounting for all cash account activity.

Question	Yes/No	Comments
Are all bank accounts reconciled within 10 days of receipt?		
Are the tasks of opening and reconciling the bank statement performed by two different people?		
Are the bank account reconciliations completed by someone other than the person who participates in the receipt or disbursement of cash?		

Do the reconciliation procedures provide for:		
Comparison of dates and amounts of deposits as shown on the bank statement with the cash receipts journal?		
Investigation of bank transfers to determine that both sides of the transactions have been recorded?		
Investigation of all bank debit and credit memos?		
Review of all checks outstanding over 90 days?		
Voiding of outstanding checks during the year end reconciliation?		
Is the bank immediately notified of all authorized check signers?		
Are all journal entries for bank charges and bank account interest recorded routinely?		

Petty cash: The following controls are meant to provide for a timely recording of expenditures of cash in the accounting system.

Question	Yes/No	Comments
Is the responsibility for the petty cash fund assigned to only one person?		
Are all petty cash funds maintained on an impress basis, i.e., the total amount of vouchers paid or disbursed, plus cash, will always equal the amount of the fund?		
Is there adequate review of documentation before the fund is reimbursed?		
Is the petty cash fund reimbursed at least monthly?		
Is the cashing of checks and loans to employees prohibited?		
Is the actual petty cash protected from theft or misplacement?		

Investments: Procedures for the proper recording and control of all investment instruments will help to assure that all assets and related income are accounted for and properly reported.

Question	Yes/No	Comments
Are all investment instruments held in the name of the church only?		
Is authorization for the sale and/or purchase of investments provided for by the church committee or authorized investment committee?		
Are all investment instruments adequately protected from fire, theft, or misplacement?		
Are the interests, dividends, and unrealized gains or losses recorded?		

Property and equipment: Certain procedures involving the physical assets of the church will aid in detecting, identifying, and preventing losses.

Question	Yes/No	Comments
Is formal approval of the church committee required for all property and equipment additions and dispositions?		
Is a detailed inventory of all property, furniture, fixtures, and equipment maintained showing:		
Date acquired?		
Detailed description?		
Cost or fair market value at time of donation?		

Any funding source restrictions?		
Is a periodic review conducted to:		
Compare the actual property, furniture and fixtures, and equipment to the recorded inventory listing?		
Ensure the adequacy of the insurance coverage?		
Improve loss prevention?		

Liabilities and other debt: All liabilities and other debt must be clearly reported, and all provisions or restrictions complied with.

Question	Yes/No	Comments
Is all borrowing or indebtedness authorized by the church committee and other appropriate committee?		
Are all loan agreements and/or lease agreements in writing and properly safeguarded?		
Are there periodic reviews conducted to determine compliance with any debt/lease provisions?		
Are all liabilities noted on Financial Statements/Reports to Church committee?		

Restricted gifts and income: Gifts restricted by donors are not handled in the same manner as other contributions, and procedures are necessary to assure that these gifts are recorded properly and all restrictions are observed.

Question	Yes/No	Comments
Are records maintained of all bequests, memorials, endowments, or any other restricted gifts to include:		
Date, amount and donor of gift?		
Any restrictions or limitations?		
Are all restricted gifts and grants approved by the Church committee or other authoritative body?		
Are the income and other transactions periodically reported to the church committee?		
Are written acknowledgements issued for all contributions other than pledges?		

Payroll: The application of policies and procedures involving the employment of individuals assures compliance with payroll tax reporting to the various governmental entities.

Question	Yes/No	Comments
Are personnel files maintained to include:		
Employment application and/or letter?		
Authorizations of pay rates & effective dates?		

Internal Revenue Service Form W-4?		
Dept. of Justice Form I-9?		
State Withholding Forms?		
Is there a written record of hours worked and approved by a supervisor when applicable?		
Are there adequate records to show computation of gross pay?		
Are there adequate records to account for all deductions from gross pay?		
Are there adequate records to support payroll tax returns and Forms W-2?		
Are payroll tax returns filed on a timely basis?		
Are payroll tax deposits made on a timely basis?		
Are all employees, clergy and lay, receiving a W-2?		
Are Forms 1099 being provided for all individuals who are not employees, and for all unincorporated entities paid $600 or more annually?		
Are Form W-2 wages reconciled to the general ledger accounts, and all four quarterly payroll tax returns?		
Are clergy house allowances recorded in the minutes of the church committee no later than the first meeting of the year?		

Computer systems: The use of computers creates the need for additional procedures to safeguard the systems and data.

Question	Yes/No	Comments
Are current or duplicate copies of the operating system and programs maintained off premises?		
Are the files backed up at least weekly and the backups maintained off premises?		
Is access to the computer and computer programs limited to authorized persons?		
Is there adequate documentation, including user manuals, available on-site for all computer programs?		
Is a printed copy retained of all journals, general ledger, financial statements and any other computerized records?		

7. SUBSTANTIVE TESTING OF TRANSACTIONS AND ACCOUNT BALANCES

Assemble the following documents:

Before assembling the documents, it should be noted that the auditor should retain a file of the work papers, which were prepared to assist with the formation of the opinion on the financial statements. When the next year's audit is to be performed, these papers could be an invaluable guide to problem areas. The next auditor, if it is not you, should be provided with a copy of your work papers. These work papers should include such things as: the marked up audit and internal control check lists; lists of bank accounts, restricted funds, investments, insurance accounts and loans; the schedules you prepared and the procedures you followed in making the audit.

Document	Yes/No	Comments
Minutes of the Church committee		
Minutes of any group authorized to disburse monies		
Annual financial report to congregation		
Treasurer's interim reports		
Names of those authorized for check signing, fund withdrawal or transfer, and disbursing approval		

List of securities held		
Copy of previous year's audit and internal control letter		
Organizational chart		
Chart of Accounts		
Budget		
General ledger		
Cash receipts journal		
Cash disbursements journal		
Bank statements for audited year, plus last statement for previous year and first for current year		
Paid checks and deposit slips		
Payroll records with Forms I-9, W-2, W-3, and State and Federal withholding records		
Savings account passbooks		
Other investment records		

Test receipts

a. *Plate offerings:* Cash receipts journal entries should be traced to weekly cash receipts records on a test basis.
b. *Pledge receipts:*
  1. An analytical test of pledges should be done as follows: determine the number of pledging units. Test the number by verifying by reference to documents generated outside of the accounting function; e.g.

membership records, directories, etc. Divide the total pledge receipts per the financial statement by the total pledging units. Compare this figure to similar records from prior periods and investigate any significant differences.

2. Adding machine tapes should be made of the individual pledge records with the total agreeing with the total pledge payments reported.

3. Random selection of individual pledge records should be tested for accurate total and balances. A minimum of 10 percent should be tested, unless number 4, below, is followed.

4. If the auditor is engaged before year end and if the church sends statements to the pledgers, the auditor can save time and effort by supervising the mailing of the year end statements. The auditor can then use this mailing to obtain direct confirmation. He does this by including a statement on the year end statements that all variances should be reported directly to the designated member of the audit committee. Any reported variances should be noted and investigated.

5. Auditors should always review the pledge receipts of the Congregation's personnel involved in money transactions.

6. The auditor should determine if any amounts should be deferred as relating to future periods; for example, in 2000, a member may make a contribution for his or her 2001 pledge. This amount should be recorded as deferred income until the year 2001. The auditor should inquire as to the existence deferred pledges and trace the deferred amount to supporting documentation.

7. Likewise, there may be pledges outstanding that were not collected by the end of the year. These should be recorded as pledges receivable. The auditor should ex-

amine the pledges in the new year to determine the adequacy of the list of pledges receivable.

The decision as to the size of the representative sample of postings and pledge records for examination depends on the dollars involved and the sophistication of the congregation's records.

c. *Contributions from mission organizations:* Receipts must be listed separately for each organization and amounts entered in the cash receipts journal traced to the weekly cash receipts records. These listed amounts shall be confirmed with their sources.

d. *Investment and endowment income:* Income from securities should be verified by an examination of the brokerage house statement. Income from investment accounts should be verified by an examination of the statements provided or confirmed by the trustee or agency. Income from savings bank deposits should be verified by examination of the entries in the savings bank passbook(s) or confirmed by the bank.

e. *Restricted income:* Income received for special purposes should be noted by the auditor who should trace the cash receipts journal entries to the weekly cash receipts records. The auditor should also be satisfied that the income was used for the purpose for which the gift was made.

f. *Non*-income receipts: Verify all cash receipts journal entries by tracing them and ascertaining that the proper authorization has been given for any transfer or inter-fund borrowing, or for the sale or redemption or any investments or property.

g. A sample of cash receipts records should be traced to duplicate deposit slips or bank statements to ascertain that these receipts are deposited intact.

h. *Petty cash:* The auditor should be satisfied that a proper impress system is being maintained. Petty cash is not to be used to cash personal checks. Cash flow and size of fund over the audit period should be checked for possible misuse.

i. All receipts should be compared to budgeted amounts and material variances should be explained.

j. Contributions of tangible assets or services. Tangible assets or services should be recorded at the fair market value of such contributions.

k. Fill out the following checklist:

Question	Yes/No	Comments
Do the records of total receipts per individual pledge agree with the amounts recorded and reported in the cash receipts journal?		
Have the postings and arithmetic on individual pledge records been tested? Number tested: _____		
Is there budgeting of contributions that can be reasonably estimated?		
Are contribution budgets periodically compared to actual, and are significant differences investigated?		

Are records kept and periodically reviewed of gifts, such as bequests, which are contingent on future events?		
Are future bequest and gift files, such as proceeds from life insurance policies or sale of property willed to a Congregation, maintained on a current basis?		
Are files kept on life income, endowment, and annuity gifts, including information on the nature of the principal, investment of the principal, or use of the principal income, as well as correspondence with donors or beneficiaries, and copies of pertinent documents?		
Are individuals designated to be responsible for assuring compliance with the terms and conditions of all grants, restricted contributions, endowments, etc. received?		

Test disbursements

a. Tests are to be made to satisfy that disbursements have been accurately classified, and that invoices in support of the disbursements have been properly approved and canceled or marked "PAID".

b. The auditor must be familiar with the financial statement expenditure categories listed on the church's chart of accounts.

c. All expense accounts should be compared to budgeted amounts and material variances should be explained.

d. Testing of Disbursements: Select a sample of disbursements in the following manner:

   i. Determine the total amount of all expenses.

   ii. Pick all disbursements with a dollar value of greater than 10% of the total expenses. For instance, if total disbursements are $100,000, any disbursement of $10,000 or more will be tested.

   iii. Pick a minimum of 60 of the remaining postings in a systematic sample. Results will indicate if a broader sampling is necessary. To choose which disbursements to test in the systematic selection, first determine the number of checks written on all accounts. Divide this number by 60. This number will be the sampling interval. For instance, if there are 2,000 checks written, you will divide this by 60, which equals 33.33. Thus, you will test every 33rd check (always round down). Therefore, if the first check number is 40, you will test check numbers 40, 73, 106, 139, and so on until you have selected 60 checks.

Make a list of the disbursements you have selected. The list should include the check number, payee, date, and amount of the check. Test as follows:

1. Compare the checks selected to the postings in the accounting records and to the accompanying invoices to determine that the disbursements are fairly recorded and classified. Comparison should include vendor's name, account classification, date, and amount billed.
2. Examine invoices for verification signature that the items were received or services performed for a sufficient number of items so the committee may be satisfied that goods and services were acknowledged by a person authorized to do so.
3. Check the arithmetic on invoices and vendors' monthly statements for a sufficient number of items to assure the committee that invoiced amounts were properly recorded on the statements.
4. Travel and business expense reimbursements should be checked to see that they are in accordance with the qualified reimbursement policy of the congregation. The auditor should examine the Church's accountable plan.

Test cash

a. The committee should ascertain a summary of the bank accounts maintained. This should include the purpose for which each is maintained.
b. The committee should examine the canceled checks for authorized signature(s) and proper endorsement.
c. The auditor should account for all voided checks.
d. The auditor should review the bank reconciliations to determine that the ending balance on the bank statement matches the one used on the reconciliation. The balance per the books should also be traced to the bank reconciliation.

e. Outstanding checks and deposits in transit from the year-end bank reconciliations should be traced to the subsequent bank statements. For instance, if you are auditing the December bank reconciliation, trace the outstanding checks to the January and February bank statements to make sure that they have cleared the bank. Any items that are left outstanding should be questioned.

f. Determine whether transfer of funds occurred between bank accounts near the balance sheet date. Determine that the transfers were recorded in the books in the same accounting period and that any transfers not recorded by the bank in the same accounting period appear in the appropriate bank reconciliation.

g. The auditor should count all petty cash accounts and reconcile the amounts to the books.

h. Fill out the following checklist:

Question	Yes/No	Comments
Is the petty cash fund imprest?		
Is the checking account(s) reconciled to the accounting records and checkbook?		
Have paid checks been examined for authorized signatures?		
Have paid checks been examined for endorsements?		
Have the checks been compared to the disbursements journal for payees and amounts?		
Have all voided checks been accounted for?		
Are checks outstanding at year-end accounted for in subsequent statements?		

Are disbursements supported by vouchers approved by authorized party other than check signer?		
Are two signatures evident on checks of $500 or more?		
Is the bank notified immediately of all changes of authorized check signers?		
Are cash journal footings tested for accuracy?		
Are receipts records compared with bank deposits?		
Are transfers between accounts traced?		
Are journal entries approved by an authorized party other than a check signer, and are they adequately documented?		
Is documentation provided to support checks written to "Cash"?		
Has the total balance of the cash summary sheet been traced to the annual financial report?		

Test investments:

a. Obtain or prepare a list of securities owned showing:
    a. The description of each security
    b. The serial number of bonds or securities
    c. The denomination of each security or its par value

d. The interest rate of each bond
e. The cost of each security and the amount recorded on the books
f. The interest and dividends received during the year
g. The market value of each bond or security as of December 31st of the year being audited
b. Review the investment summary for reasonableness, consistency of amounts between years and obvious omissions.
c. Compare the securities listed with ledger accounts and/or with the brokerage statement. Whenever practicable serial numbers should be compared with records of security purchases in order to obtain positive identification and to avoid the possibility of substitution.
d. Examine securities listed or obtain confirmation from the holders if any are held by depositories. It is preferable for this examination to occur as close to the examination date as possible. Insure that the securities are registered in the name of the church or are endorsed as to be transferrable to the church. Examine the coupons on bonds to ascertain that un-matured coupons are intact.
e. Examine all transactions for verification of acquisitions and disposition.
f. Trace acquisitions to disbursement records and sales (dispositions) to receipts records.
g. Examine broker statements and compare with investment ledger where applicable.
h. The auditor should be satisfied that the securities are being adequately safeguarded.
i. Examine securities for ownership, certificate number, dates, endorsements, assignments, etc.
j. Verify any income, which has not yet been distributed.
k. Determine, by reference to dates of purchase and disposal of investments, interest rates and published dividend rec-

ords, whether income earned and accrued income receivable has been appropriately recorded.

l. Fill out the following checklist:

Question	Yes/No	Comments
Is the securities list verified against subsidiary ledger accounts, validating serial numbers against purchase records of gifts?		
Is the name in which securities are registered verified?		
In the case of coupon bonds, are un-matured coupons intact?		
Is the market value of securities established at the date of the examination?		
Are securities examined, or confirmed if held by depository or transfer agent?		
Are brokers reports examined for securities bought or sold through brokers?		
Were security purchases or sales authorized by appropriate church committee action and recorded in the minutes?		

Have cash receipts records of dividends and interest been compared with record of securities held?		
Have the investments been recorded at their fair market value?		
Has the total balance of the summary of investments (recorded at fair value) been traced to the financial report?		

Test trust and endowment funds:

a. Obtain or prepare a list of trust and endowment funds showing:
   a. The source and date;
   b. Terms governing the use of principal and income;
   c. To whom and how often reports of condition are to be made; and
   d. How the funds are to be invested
b. Examine the trust or agency agreement for each new trust and endowment fund received during the fiscal year.
c. Fill out the following checklist:

Question	Yes/No	Comments
Has a list of trust and endowment funds been obtained, including their terms and locations of the investments?		

Has there been an examination of the deed of trust or agency agreement for each trust and endowment fund?		
Have the agency accounting records been checked to determine whether or not the terms of the trust or endowment funds are being properly followed?		
Have the endowment funds been recorded at their fair market values?		
Has the total balance of the endowment fund summary (recorded at fair value) been traced to the financial report?		

Test debt:

a. Obtain or prepare a schedule of all loans to include:
    a. The name of the lending institution
    b. The date or origin
    c. The original amount of loan
    d. The interest rate and payment schedule
    e. The monthly payment
    f. The unpaid balance
    g. The purpose of loan
    h. The authorizing body
    i. The collateral for the loan
    j. The restrictions placed by the lender

b. Review balances for reasonableness, consistency of amounts between years and obvious omissions.

c. Determine that any loans from the year being examined had the proper authorization and were recorded in the minutes of the church committee.

d. Verify, by direct communication with any lender, the outstanding indebtedness.

e. Reconcile the unpaid balance of all loans as reported by the church records to the figure reported by the lending institution.

f. Fill out the following checklist:

Question	Yes/No	Comments
Has all indebtedness been properly authorized by appropriate church officials?		
Have unpaid balances per church records been reconciled with balances as reported by creditor?		
Is a detailed schedule of all loans prepared, including name of creditor, date of origin, original amount of debt, interest rate payment schedule, monthly payment, unpaid balance, loan purpose, and authorizing body?		
Has the total from the detailed schedule been traced to the financial report?		

Test property and equipment

a. Obtain a list of fixed assets showing the cost or fair market value, if donated, and date of purchase.
b. Review balances for reasonableness, consistency of amounts between years, and obvious omissions.
c. Examine all the deeds and titles of ownership related to the properties owned by the congregation. Review them for the proper recording of the name of the owner and to determine if any encumbrances or liens exist.
d. Determine if any inventory identification procedure is in effect.
e. The church must have a physical inventory of capital assets. A sampling test of this inventory is to be made by the auditor.
f. Ensure that all property and equipment is adequately insured.
g. If depreciation of property is recognized, review entries for accuracy.
h. Fill out the following checklist:

Question	Yes/No	Comments
Is there a list of fixed assets, showing date of purchase and cost?		
Is an inventory identification procedure in effect?		
Using preceding information, has a physical examination of assets been made, to extent possible?		
Have any deeds and titles required been examined as evidence of ownership?		
Are land and buildings carried on financial statements?		

Are any liens outstanding against any property and equipment?		
Has the total of the detailed schedule been traced to the financial report?		

Test payroll:

a. Examine the individual earnings records for name, address, social security number, number of exemptions, rate of pay, and effective date.

b. Ensure that the salary paid is authorized and proper by comparing with the amount budgeted.

c. Trace the individual earnings record postings to the check register.

d. Reconcile total wages paid and total withholding taxes with the quarterly Form 941 and end-of-year Form W-3, checking that they were remitted on time.

e. Determine if a current signed federal form W-4 and a form I-9 is on file for each employee hired after November 6, 1986.

f. Determine if a Form W-2 has been given to each employee (including clergy) and that the Forms W-2 are correct and properly filed.

g. Determine if Forms 1099 are being provided for all individuals who are not employees and unincorporated entities paid $600 or more annually and all recipients of educational scholarship funds of $3,000 or more in a given year.

h. Test the payroll to be sure that a real employee exists for every payroll check written.

i. Fill out the following checklist:

Question	Yes/No	Comments
Have total wages been reconciled with quarterly Federal Form 941, Form W-2, and Form W-3?		
Have total withholding taxes been reconciled with Form 941?		
Has it been determined that all Federal and State withholding taxes were remitted on a timely basis, to avoid hidden penalties?		
Is a current signed Form W-4 on hand for each employee?		
Has the total balance of the payroll reconciliation been traced to the financial report?		

Test receivables and payables:

a. Prepare a schedule of accounts receivable as of the balance sheet date. These may include pledge payments which were made after the end of the year in which they money was pledged or authentic obligations owed to the congregation at year end. Check the cash receipts in the new year to verify that the amounts listed were collected. Inquire as to any uncollected balances.

b. Prepare a schedule of payables as of the balance sheet date. These may include monies owed by the congregation to vendors at year-end for goods and services received during the year being audited. Look in the paid bills file for the new year and trace any invoices dated in the year under examination to the accounts payable listing. For example, if you are auditing the 1999 payable figure, ask the treasurer for the file of the January 2000 bills in which he or she paid. Examine these invoices to see if they are dated for 1999. If they are dated 1999, but not paid until 2000, they should be on the payables list.

Also examine the new year's cash disbursement journal and search for any liabilities which have not been recorded. Discuss with the treasurer any old or disputed payables.

c. Fill out the following checklist:

Question	Yes/No	Comments
Is there a policy covering the procedure for write-offs of receivables or loans, approval required, provision for reserves?		
Have the items on the payable and receivable lists been traced to subsequent payments or deposits?		
Have the totals of the detailed payable and receivable schedules been traced to the financial report?		

Test net assets:

A schedule should be prepared listing net assets according to the following classifications: unrestricted, temporarily restricted, and permanently restricted. All restrictions should be reviewed and verified. The summary schedules should be traced to the financial report.

Test insurance:

A schedule should be prepared listing the name of carrier, description of coverage, period of coverage, period of insurance, premium amount and date of premium payment for the following policies which the committee is to review:

a. Fire insurance on building and equipment
b. General Liability (Public Liability and Property Damage)
c. Burglary
d. Fine Arts
e. Malpractice
f. Workmen's Compensation
g. Fidelity Bond
h. Automobile coverage on cars owned by the church
i. Non-ownership liability insurance for cars owned by others when used for church business.
j. Directors' and Officers' Liability
k. Umbrella Liability
l. Other special policies held by the church
m. Fill out the following checklist:

Question	Yes/No	Comments
Has insurance coverage been reviewed, and has a copy of policies been obtained and a schedule prepared detailing name of carrier, description of coverage, period covered, premium amount, and date of premium payment?		

Has there been inquiry as to whether there are any contingencies facing the church, e.g., legal action with prospects of potential loss?		

Test the discretionary fund:

Check that the discretionary fund is in the name of the church, that the church's federal tax identification number is the number used to identify the account at the bank, and that the fund has not been used for operating fund expenses or for the personal expenses of the clergy. If a separate checking account has been authorized, all monies for the discretionary fund must pass through the church's general bank account and subsequently a check should be written to transfer the monies to the separate discretionary fund checking account.

8. AUDITOR'S WRITTEN REPORT

The type of report provided at the conclusion of the audit will be dependent on the type of audit performed. For agreed upon procedure and financial statement audits performed by an independent CPA, professional audit standards will dictate the reporting providing by the auditor.

For audits performed by church member, the reporting ideally will provide the following, at a minimum:

1. Listing of Procedures Performed and Related Results
2. Statement of Financial Position (balance sheet or listing of all assets and liabilities if full financial statements are not prepared for the church)
3. Statement of changes in net assets (statement of activities or listing of all income and expenses if full financial statements are not prepared for the church)
4. Comments, if any, on internal control deficiencies or issues with church procedures noted during the evaluation.

The reporting should be provided in written format to the audit committee (or finance committee if there is no audit committee) to disclose the results of testing and any findings or observations during the audit.

Preparing the Audit Report

While the audit report is in draft format, the auditor should meet with the audit or finance committee to discuss the audit report. The final audit report, along with any responses the finance committee may choose to add, should then be delivered to the Church.

Although church meetings generally must be open to all, discussions with accountants and matters involving personnel issues may be held in closed meetings if confidential information is likely to be disclosed. Examples of discussions that should happen in closed session include, but are not limited to, suspicion of inappropriate use of church funds or embezzlement. Suspicions should not be discussed in open meetings. Closed meetings will include only the members of the committee that is meeting, plus any invited guests, such as the auditor or the church's legal advisor.

When the auditor has delivered the audit to the church with responses of the finance committee, the audit process is finished for that fiscal year. The auditor's findings and Report of the Annual Audit should be kept by the church permanently. The reports should be provided to the subsequent year's audit team for review in preparation for the next audit.

The Audit Report

All of the work of the Audit Committee will yield very limited benefits unless the results are communicated to the church leadership and membership. This final step is accomplished in the form of an audit report signed by the members of the Audit Committee and attached to the annual financial reports of the church.

While the exact language of the report may vary from church to church, it should consider the following:

1) The subject of the audit report, namely the annual financial reports;
2) What the Committee did, namely audit the records and reports;
3) The limitations of the Committee's work, namely that it is not a guarantee of accuracy; and
4) An opinion on the fairness of the records and reports.

The Committee may also wish to include in its report a word of commendation for the tireless work of the church treasurer and financial secretary. This would certainly be in the Christian spirit of lifting up the efforts of these individuals before the congregation they serve. A sample audit report is presented below.

Report of the Audit Committee

Date:

To: The Church Leadership and Membership

We have audited the records and financial reports of First Church of Anytown dated xx/xx/xxxx and contained herein. While our audit was limited to testing the transactions and balances and would not necessarily disclose all errors, we found no evidence of significant errors or omissions. In our opinion, the financial reports mentioned above are fairly stated.

We wish to commend the treasurer, financial secretary, and assistant treasurer for their fine work during the year. On behalf of the congregation, we thank them for the gift of their time and talent.

_____   _____
John Smith – Auditor   Mary Jones – Auditor

December 2010 Audit

DATE

I. ORGANIZATION

Church is a not-for-profit organization existing under the laws of the State. The vestry is responsible for the preparation and fair presentation of the financial statements in accordance with the cash basis of accounting and for the designing, implementing, and maintaining internal control relevant to the preparation and fair presentation of the financial statements.

The parish administrator is responsible for entering all the case receipts and cash disbursements in the system and the preparation of the monthly financial statements. Before the financial statements are presented to the vestry, the Vestry Treasurer reviews them.

The last audit of the fiscal year 2009 had the following recommendations:

- It was recommended that the treasurers' report be expanded in its analysis and follow-up of vestry approved special expenditures be noted in the treasurers' report. Additionally the administrative secretary and secretary to the vestry must establish a procedure for adequate filing and storage of vestry meeting minutes.

  o *Per the treasurer and head of the finance committee, this recommendation has been implemented. We reviewed the vestry minutes and they were filed in a binder.*

The following observations and recommendations are from the 2010 audit:

II. FINDINGS

Bank Account

- At year-end, there were two bank accounts with Anytown Bank. An Operating account and a Designated fund account. Both accounts are reconciled in QuickBooks and the proper reconciliation reports are attached to the bank statements. Both accounts were off by $6.00 in December. The difference is the result of a bank transfer made to correct a deposit but the book transfer was not done. The error was corrected the following month.
- It was noted that on several occasions the bank reconciliation was not done until two months after the statement date.
  - o Bank statements need to be reconciled as soon as received. This will ensure any discrepancies or errors are corrected immediately.
- There were two instances where bank transfers were done however; there was no description or authorization for the transfer.
  - o All transfers need to be documented and authorized.
- An individual who does not have signature authority on the checking accounts reconciles the bank statements however; the reconciliations were not approved and signed by the Vestry Treasurer.
  - o All bank reconciliations accounts should be reviewed and signed by the Vestry Treasurer.

Cash Receipts

- The church utilizes two systems. The ACS People module is used to track and record all contributions and pledges. QuickBooks is used for the financial accounting. The totals from the ACS proof report are entered into QuickBooks as Cash receipts
- Count sheets are completed however only for cash deposits.
  - Noted three instances (out of 15 tested) where the count sheet was not filled out correctly. The cash amount was written on the total check line instead of the cash line. It is important that the count sheets be filled out correctly and signed by both counters.
  - Listing checks on the count sheet as opposed to photocopying them would reduce copying costs and increase efficiency.

Disbursements

- The church's policy is to have two signers on every check. All checks written out of the operating account were reviewed.
  - There were 25 instances in the Operating account where the check did not have two signatures. It is important that the policies implemented by followed.
- All checks written out of the designated account were reviewed.
  - There were 10 instances where the check did not have two signatures.

Investments

- In July, the Endowment Account CD for $10,408.36 was closed and the funds transferred into the operating account.
  - The motion for approval to close the account and transfer the funds into the operating account could not be located in the vestry minutes.

Restricted Accounts

- Temporarily restricted net assets consist of gifts available for the following:

215 Special Church Funds	501.95
21509 Salvador Fund	552.49
2151 Ladies of Church	920.93
21510 Altar Guild Fund	28.24
21514 Men of Church	100.00
21516 Africa Mission Fund	60.00
21517 Vacation Bible School	337.83
2152 Youth Fund	1,072.53
2154 Acolyte Attire Fund	269.03
2155 Music Fund	400.00
2158 Building Fund	898.00
21591 Flower Fund	412.00
21592 Memorial Fund	1,300.00
21955 Clergy Gifts	456.00
21957 Outreach Fund	175.00
21958 Bookstore	1,072.03
21960 Organ Fund	1,691.00
21961 Preschool Fund	0.00
21963 Fellowship Fund	2,130.17
21964 Sabbatical Fund	0.00

```
21965 Mission Trip                    114.00
21966 Misc. Deposit Fund            2,000.00
Total 215 Special Church Funds      $xxxxxx
```

- The cash account associated with the restricted assets is $xx,xxx.00. There is a $130.00 difference between the cash account and the restricted funds. The difference needs to be researched.

Payroll

- The church had four employees on the payroll at year-end. No discrepancies were found relating to payroll. All quarterly reports were filed. The Payroll Tax Payable of $xxx.35 on the balance sheet at yearend was payable in January 2011 however there is $434 in accrued payroll taxes on the balance sheet that could not be verified. A journal entry should be done to clear the account.

Debt

- May 21, 2010 a cash receipt for $ xx,xxx.00 was received and deposited into the operating account. The deposit was miscoded in QuickBooks. The deposit was recorded as miscellaneous income however the deposit was actually a loan. An entry needs to be made to reclassify the $13,000 from miscellaneous income on the profit and loss statement to a liability account on the balance sheet.
- May 9, 2008 church modified a $ xx,xxx.00 loan, which had an outstanding balance of $ xx,xxx.00 with Anytown Florida Bank. The Note was extended until May 5, 2013 at 6.89% interest. The loan

shall be due and payable for $ xx,xxx.00 commencing on June 5, 2008 and continuing on the same day of each month thereafter until fully paid. The balance sheet does not agree to the yearend statement from the bank. A journal entry for the difference of $ xx,xxx.00 should be made on the books to reconcile the balance.

▪ Church signed two promissory notes on July 1, 2002 with XXXX. The original balances on the notes were $ xx,xxx.00 and $ xx,xxx.00. The loan on the balance sheet is split between three accounts. It is recommended that all three accounts be consolidated into one. Additionally the amounts do not reflect the true amount owed at the year-end. The total owed including past due apportionments for 2008, 2009, and 2010 is $392,371.00. An entry needs to be done to correct the balance.

Total confirmed debt at December 31, 2010 is as follows:

- ▪ Note Payable   13,000.00
- ▪ Note Payable Diocese   392,371.00
- ▪ Anytown Florida Bank   <u>404,995.42</u>

     Total Debt   <u>$xxx,xxx</u>

▪ There is $xxx,xxx in the Accounts Payable Clearing account on the balance sheet, which needs to be researched and cleaned up.

Pledges

- No findings. The church utilizes ACS People to track all pledges and contributions. All individuals are given a number that corresponds to the number on their pledge envelopes.

Fixed Assets

- A fixed asset listing that included balances was provided out of QuickBooks. There needs to be a more detailed listing of the assets listed on the balance sheet. There also needs to be a procedure in place for the acquisition and disposal of assets.

III. INTERNAL CONTROL RECOMMENDATIONS

- The Accounting Policy and Procedures manual should be completed. This will help with all future audits.
- All balance sheet accounts need to be reconciled every month. This will catch any errors that may have been made and ensure that all balances are correct.
- The bank statement and bank reconciliation need to be signed and reviewed by the treasurer every month.
- The church should consider reducing the requirement amount on checks needing two signatures to maybe $500.00. The policy now is that all checks require two signatures however obtaining two signatures seems to be a problem.

- The monthly financials presented should reflect the actual financial data compared with the approved budget.
- The church needs to have a detail listing of all assets at a minimum for insurance purposes.

Glossary

A local church audit - an independent evaluation of the financial reports and records of the internal controls of the local church by a qualified person or persons for the purpose of reasonably verifying the reliability of financial reporting, determining whether assets are being safeguarded, and whether the law, and policies and procedures are being complied with.

Audit - the term is meant to be a process that provides reasonable assurance that good stewardship is being used in handling and accounting for the funds and other assets of the local church. The ultimate goals of the audit include:

- Protection for the persons the local church elects to offices of financial responsibility from unwarranted charges of careless or improper handling of funds;
- Trust and confidence of the financial supporters of the church in the way their money is being accounted for (trust and confidence lead to improved patterns of financial support);
- Fiscal responsibility to assure that through turnover of personnel there will be continuity in accountability and transparency;
- Assurance that gifts made to the church with restrictions attached are consistently administered in accordance with the donors' instructions and to provide checks and balances for funds received and expended.

Designated funds - assets that have been voted by the local church's governing board, such as its church, council or equivalent body, to be used for a particular purpose. Because the stipulation for its particular use was made by the church itself, that stipulation (or designation) can be changed by the action of the body that put it in place.

Imprest - A loan, usually in the form of a petty cash account, that can be drawn on as needed.

Independent Audit - Independent means that the auditor must not be subject to control or influence by anyone who has responsibility for the financial accounts and records of the local church. There should not be even the appearance of a relationship that may dilute the perception of the independence of the auditor. An independent auditor is one who is unrelated to those with financial responsibilities in the church. If a CPA or accounting firm is chosen, the firm should be unrelated and separate from those with financial responsibilities in the church.

Internal controls - policies and procedures that are followed to help minimize financial risks by helping to deter potential fraud, detect errors or omissions and protect innocent workers.

Internal control policy - a policy prepared for a church that documents the processes and procedures to be followed to help safeguard the financial assets of the church.

Permanently restricted funds - donations to the church for a particular purpose where the original gift is not spent but the earnings on the gift can be used for that purpose.

Temporarily restricted funds - donations to the church that come with stipulations that limit the use of the funding to a specified purpose. The funding can be spent but just for the intended purpose.

Unrestricted funds - donations made to the church that are for the general use in the ministry of the church.

Other Books:

THE Minister's Handbook: *A Guide for Leadership*

Preaching that Empowers God's People: *Expository Preaching in the 21st Century*

A Pastor's Introduction to Church Administration: *Administering the 21st Century Church Effectively*